RIPENING

"*Oneing*" is an old English word that was used by Lady Julian of Norwich (1342–1416) to describe the encounter between God and the soul. The Rohr Institute proudly borrows the word to express the divine unity that stands behind all of the divisions, dichotomies, and dualisms in the world. We pray and publish with Jesus' words, "that all may be one" (John 17:21).

EDITOR: Vanessa Guerin
PUBLISHER: The Center for Action and Contemplation

ADVISORY BOARD:
David Benner
James Danaher
Ilia Delio, OSF
Sheryl Fullerton
Marion Küstenmacher

EDITORIAL COMMITTEE:
Richard Rohr, OFM
Alicia Johnson
Vanessa Guerin
Matt Sholler

Design and Composition by Nelson Kane Design

Wood engraving by David Klein

Oneing

VOLUME 1 NO. 2

EDITOR'S NOTE

The purpose of life in a society such as ours is to ward off death, keep hair from greying at all costs, and hide wrinkles. It is a sterile land, full of fraud, steeped in the superficial, and bereft of the real tastes and lessons of life.
—Joan Chittister

T HERE WAS A TIME when family elders were revered as wisdom keepers. They were the ones who held the life experiences that made them the honored storytellers and cornerstones of the family. Unfortunately, today's wisdom keepers are often shut off from society, kept in "homes" where others, besides family members, can care for them. Out of sight, out of mind!

But these elders were young once. Many lived through the Great Depression and survived several wars, the births, celebrations, and deaths of family members, financial gains and losses, joys and sorrows. As Abraham Joshua Heschel writes so poignantly, "Old age is not a defeat, but a victory, not a punishment but a privilege. The test of a people is how it behaves toward the old...."

Life stages are a lot like ripening fruit—the body, mind and spirit develop over the course of time, from an early "green" stage; to subtle changes in color, ripeness, and juiciness; to rich fullness; before becoming old, withered and falling to the ground. Through each of these stages of maturation, we do have opportunities for inner growth.

In this edition of *Oneing* we come to understand the sanctity of the ripening process from master teachers who offer us ways to "learn to live well," as Joan Chittister teaches, while, as Joe Grant states, "growing down to earth." Each article, beginning with Richard Rohr's insightful introduction, invites us to slowly savor, then pause and reflect before moving on to the next.

Vanessa Guerin,
Editor

CONTRIBUTORS

Richard Rohr, OFM, is a Franciscan of the New Mexico Province and the Founding Director of the Center for Action and Contemplation (CAC) in Albuquerque, New Mexico, home of the Rohr Institute. An internationally-recognized author and spiritual leader, Father Richard teaches primarily on incarnational mysticism, non-dual consciousness, and contemplation, with a particular emphasis on how these affect the social justice issues of our time. Along with many recorded conferences, he is the author of numerous books, including his newly-released collection of daily meditations, *Yes, And...*. To learn more about Father Richard Rohr and the CAC, visit cac.org.

Chris Ellery, PhD, a member of the Texas Institute of Letters, is Professor of English at Angelo State University, where he teaches American literature, film criticism, and creative writing. Dr. Ellery is the author of three books of poetry, most recently *The Big Mosque of Mercy*, which includes poems based on his experiences in the Middle East, including Syria, where he was a Fulbright lecturer. To learn more about Chris Ellery, please visit angelo.edu.

Joan Chittister, OSB, PhD, a Benedictine Sister of Erie, Pennsylvania, is a best-selling author and well-known international lecturer on topics of justice, peace, human rights, women's issues, and contemporary spirituality in the church and in society. She presently serves as the co-chair of the Global Peace Initiative of Women, a partner organization of the United Nations, facilitating a worldwide network of women peace builders, especially in the Middle East. Sister Joan has written numerous books, including *Following the Path: The Search for a Life of Passion, Purpose and Joy*. She is Executive Director of Benetvision, a resource for contemporary spirituality. To learn more about Sister Joan Chittister, visit benetvision.org.

Joe Grant, MDiv, a native of Scotland, received a Masters of Divinity from Catholic Theological Union in Chicago. After working among indigenous people in the Amazon and North America, Joe now lives in inner-city Louisville with his wife and three children. He serves as a program writer for JustFaith Ministries and is the developer of the Engaging Spirituality process. To learn more about Joe Grant, visit justfaith.org.

Sally K. Severino, MD, is an author, speaker, and Professor Emeritus of Psychiatry at the University of New Mexico Health Sciences Center. Grounded in the Christian contemplative tradition, she is a Felician Associate of the Assumption of the Blessed Virgin Mary. Dr. Severino, together with Dr. Nancy Morrison, is the author of *Sacred Desire: Growing in Compassionate Living*. To learn more about Sally K. Severino, visit templetonpress.org.

James Finley, PhD, lived as a monk at the cloistered Trappist monastery of the Abbey of Gethsemani in Kentucky, where the world-renowned monk and author, Thomas Merton, was his spiritual director. A clinical psychologist in private practice, and a retreat and workshop leader, James Finley is the author of several books on contemplative prayer, including *Merton's Palace of Nowhere*. To learn more about James Finley, visit contemplativeway.org.

Kathleen Dowling Singh, PhD, a dharma practitioner and transpersonal psychologist, is the author of *The Grace in Dying: How We are Transformed Spiritually as We Die*. "Living in the Light of Death" is adapted from *The Grace in Aging*, to be published by Wisdom Publications in 2014. To learn more about Kathleen Dowling Singh, visit kathleendowlingsingh.com.

Tilden Edwards, PhD, an Episcopal priest, is Founder and Senior Fellow of The Shalem Institute. He served as Shalem's Executive Director from 1979 until 2000, and continues to be involved in several of Shalem's programs. Dr. Edwards is the author or editor of numerous books, including *Embracing the Call to Spiritual Depth: Gifts for Contemplative Living*. To learn more about Tilden Edwards, visit shalem.org.

MARK T. MCGONIGLE, MAS, LCSW, is the owner of Wise Mind Therapy Services in Kansas City, Missouri, where he provides psychotherapy, specializing in couples counseling and treatment of trauma. He is the creator of the "Fix a Fight" iPhone app (seen on the "Today Show" and in *The New York Times*, *Redbook*, and *Time Magazine*), which helps couples repair intimacy after regrettable interactions. To learn more about Mark McGonigle, visit markmcgonigle.com.

JOELLE CHASE is Director of Messaging at the Center for Action and Contemplation, helping to craft words that convey the great Mystery (though it can never be fully captured or known through language). Joelle and her husband, Peter, live on a small urban homestead in Albuquerque, New Mexico, where they seek to live more simply and sustainably. Together they look forward to ripening naturally, in God's good time.

HARRY R. MOODY, PHD, has recently retired as Vice President and Director of Academic Affairs for AARP in Washington, DC. He is currently Visiting Professor at Tohoku University in Japan, and Distinguished Visiting Professor at Fielding Graduate University. The editor of the newsletter *Human Values in Aging*, Dr. Moody is the author of numerous books, including *The Five Stages of the Soul: Charting the Spiritual Passages That Shape Our Lives*, which has been translated into seven languages.

W. ANDREW ACHENBAUM, PHD, is Professor of History and Social Work at the University of Houston, and serves as chair of the National Council on the Aging and several Federal and philanthropic blue ribbon panels. Dr. Achenbaum, the author of *Old Age in the New Land: The American Experience since 1790*, specializes in the history of aging, ranging from images to policymaking to spirituality. To learn more about W. Andrew Auchenbaum, visit uh.edu.

INTRODUCTION

The life and death of a human being is so exquisitely calibrated
as to automatically produce union with Spirit.
— Kathleen Dowling Singh

W E CHOSE THE WORD "ripening" for the theme of the second issue of *Oneing* to move us beyond any exclusive concern with physical aging. Our concerns are much broader than that. We want to talk about notions of maturity, elder-ship, staging, sequencing, growth, and direction. Where is this thing we call "life" headed? Who sets the standard? Is there any standard?

Beginning with Jesus' four kinds of soil and receptivity (Mt 13:4–9), to John of the Cross' "nights" and Teresa of Avila's "mansions," through the modern schemas of Jean Piaget, James Fowler, Lawrence Kohlberg, Eric Erickson, Abraham Maslow, Carol Gilligan, and Bill Plotkin, each clarify that there is a clear direction and staging to maturity and therefore to human life. We live inside of some kind of coherence and purpose, a believer might say.

Unless we can somehow chart this trajectory, we have no way to discern growth or maturity, and no ability to discern what might be a full, fuller, or fullest human response. Neither do we have any criteria for discerning an immature, regressive, or even sick response. When pluralism itself becomes the goal, a postmodern dilemma is created. There must be a direction to ripening, but we must also recognize that *any steps toward maturity are by necessity immature.* An understanding of ripening basically teaches us the wisdom of timing, love, and patience, and allows us to be wise instead of judgmental.

Having said that, and if I am to believe the novels, myths, poems, and people that I have met in my life, old age is almost never described as an apex of achievement, hardly ever sitting atop a summit with the raised arms of a victorious athlete. It is something else, almost always something else—usually something other than what was initially imagined, or even hoped for.

Ripening reveals much bigger or very different horizons than we realize. The refusal to ripen leads to what T.S. Eliot spoke of in "The Hollow Men," lives that "end not with a bang but with a whimper." I trust that you are one of those who will move toward your own endless horizons and not waste time in whimpering. Why else would you even read this article? Perhaps this issue of *Oneing* may help you trust that you are, in fact, being led. Life—your life, all life—is going somewhere, and somewhere good. You do not need to navigate the river, for you are already flowing within it.

Ripening, at its best, is a slow, patient learning, and sometimes even a happy letting-go—a seeming emptying out to create readiness for a new kind of fullness—which we are never sure about. If we do not allow our own ripening, and I do believe it is somewhat of a natural process,[1] an ever-increasing resistance and denial sets in, an ever-increasing circling of the wagons around an over-defended self. At our very best, we learn how to hope as we ripen, to move outside and beyond self-created circles, which is something quite different from the hope of the young. Youthful hopes have concrete goals, whereas the hope of older years is usually aimless hope, hope without goals, even naked hope—perhaps real hope.

Such stretching is the agony and the joy of later years, although one can avoid both of these rich experiences too. Old age, as such, is almost a complete changing of gears and engines from the first half of our lives, and does not happen without many slow realizations, inner calmings, lots of inner resistance and denials too, and eventual surrenders, *all of them* by God's grace working with our ever deepening sense of what we really desire and who we really are.. This process seems to largely operate unconsciously, although we jolt into consciousness now and then, and the *awareness that you have been led, often despite yourself,* is experienced as a deep gratitude that most would call happiness.

This movement is the natural and organic inner work of the second half of our lives, especially if we are granted the full "70 years, or 80 if we are strong" (Ps 90:10). Of course, for many the whole process of ripening, and the deepening of desire, is cut short by a tragic, untimely death. Yet we have all seen much younger people accelerate the entire process through an early, perhaps fatal, illness. (If the dying process occurs consciously, it is an extremely accelerated ripening, as in a hot house.) Why would any of us ripen until it is demanded of us? For some the demand comes early. Maybe God knows that most of the rest of us are slow learners and need more time to ripen.

Reality, fate, destiny, providence, and tragedy are slow but insistent teachers. The horizon of old age seems to be a plan that God has prepared as inevitable and part of the necessary school of life. What is gratuitously given is also gratuitously taken away, just as Job slowly came to accept. And sometimes we remember that his final pained response was "Blessed be the name of the Lord!" (Jb 1:21). We all live in the same cycle of unrequested birth and unrequested death. Someone else is clearly in control, yet most of our lives are spent accepting and surrendering to this truth, and in trusting that this "someone" is good and trustworthy besides. It is the very shape of faith and the entire journey of faith.

If we are to speak of a *spirituality* of ripening, we need to recognize that it is always (and I do mean *always*) characterized by an increasing tolerance for ambiguity, a growing sense of subtlety, an ever-larger ability to include and allow, and a capacity to live with contradictions and even to love them! I cannot imagine any other way of coming to those broad horizons except through many trials, unsolvable paradoxes, and errors in trying to resolve them.

Without such a gradually-renewed mind and heart, we almost certainly will end with a whimper — not just our own, but also the whimpering of those disappointed souls gathered around our sick bed or gravestone. Too many lives have indeed been lives of "quiet desperation" and God must surely rush to console and comfort all humans before, during, and after their passing. Many put off enlightenment as long as they can. Maybe this whole phenomenon is what Catholics actually mean by purgatory. Without such after-death hope, I would go crazy with sadness at all the lives which appear to end so *unripened*. The All-Merciful One is surely free to show mercy even after we die. Why would God be all-loving before death but not after death? Isn't it the same God? I've seen no one die perfectly "whole." We are all saved by mercy, "wound round and round," as Merton said. Some do appear to *float into pure love* in their very final days among us.

A ripening mind and heart is most basically a capacity for non-dual consciousness and contemplation. Many might just call it a growth in compassion, but surely no growth in compassion is likely unless one learns how to forgive as a very way of life, and to let go of almost everything as we first imagined it *had to be*. This is possible as we grow in the more truly Jewish, and eventually Christian, notion of faith, where not-knowing (the *apophatic* way) must be carefully paired with knowing (the *kataphatic* way). The Judeo-Christian tradition balanced our so-called knowing with *trust, patience, allowing, waiting, humility, love*, and *forgiveness*, which is very nearly the entire message, and surely the core message, necessary for the possibility of ripening. Otherwise, we all close down, and history freezes up with all of its hurts, memories, and resentments intact.

Non-dual consciousness was largely lost after the in-house fighting of the Christian reformations (16th century) and the defensive posturing of the Enlightenment (17th and 18th centuries).[2] Henceforth we thought we had to *know* or, at least, pretend that we *did know*, to prove the others wrong. We deemed full certitude as a total need, and even a right and obligation! How strange and impossible it is when you think about it.

We now study the Scriptures, but only with great difficulty do we share in the actual consciousness of Abraham, Sarah, Moses, Job, Jesus, and the many Marys of the New Testament. They became pious stories of an idyllic time rather than reflecting a level of consciousness. In between, there have been thousands of years of history, religious reformations, and rational thinking. For the most part, we no longer "understand spiritual things in a spiritual way" (1 Cor 2:13) — which is truly the only way to understand them. A non-dual way of knowing in the moment gives us a life *process* and not simply momentary dualistic answers, which always grow old because they are never totally true.

So my guidance, in this lovely issue of *Oneing*, is a simple reminder and recall to what we will be forced to learn by necessity and under pressure anyway — the *open-ended way of allowing* and the *deep meaning* that some call faith. To live in trustful faith is to ripen; it is almost that simple. Let's start practicing now, early in our life, so we do not have to take a crash course in our final years, weeks, and days. The best ripening happens naturally over time.

Richard Rohr, OFM

The Ripe and the Unripe Fruit

The unripe can't understand what it feels like
to be ready.
—Jalaluddin Rumi

In the season of sweet melon and cantaloupe,
The grapes cannot know their own luscious ripeness,
The heavy readiness to let go of the vine.

The green wheat, just beginning to sprout,
Like some poor child, all vanity and ego,
Thinks it wants to be young forever.

When pistachios crackle open
By moonlight, they are joyfully sighing,
Why did we not know?

Learning to Live Well for the Sake of Those Who Have Yet Lived Little

By Joan Chittister, OSB, PhD

A MONG THE SAYINGS or "words" of the Desert Monastics, one story piques a new kind of spiritual interest in the issue of aging. The story reads: a monk once came to Basil of Caesarea and said, "Speak a word, Father." Basil replied, "Thou shalt love the Lord thy God with all thy heart," and the monk went away at once. Twenty years later he came back and said, "Father, I have struggled to keep your word, now speak another word to me." Basil said, "Thou shalt love thy neighbor as thyself," and the monk returned in obedience to his cell to that also.

Life, the story seems to say, is not simply a series of events, a checklist of answers. It is a deepening of insights from one stage of life to another, from one period of readiness to another, from one phase of responsibility and growth to another. Life, in other words, is learned in stages and layers and levels, each of them deeper than the one before it. Age, in this story, is not lived in discrete events. It is one continuous movement from womb to tomb.

Life, then, is the enrichment of the self from one moment to the next, each of which informs the other, until finally, having reflected on them all, lived all of them through to the last ounce of presence and perception, the adult emerges in us, whole and entire, a spiritual model for all to see.

> Or, to put it another way, in a youth-centered culture apples never ripen and fall from trees, giant Redwoods never age, mountains never wear down, and children never grow up. Everything is static. Everything is simply episodic. Nothing changes. Nothing matures. Nothing dies out or becomes more of itself. In a television age, eternal youth is the goal. Nothing grows from one stage into another. The purpose of life in a society such as ours is to ward off death, keep hair from greying at all costs, and hide wrinkles. It is a sterile land, full of fraud, steeped in the superficial, and bereft of the real tastes and lessons of life.

At the end of the epic poem, "Ulysses," Tennyson says it best. While we hear in the muted background the noise of a civilization determined to drown out the truth of it all, he simply refuses to ignore the underlying truth of age and instead sings of the depth and purpose of the progression of years. He writes:

Though much is taken, much abides; and though
We are not now that strength which in old days
Moved earth and heaven, that which we are, we are;
One equal temper of heroic hearts,
Made weak by time and fate, but strong in will
To strive, to seek, to find, and not to yield.[1]

From this perspective, the problem with contemporary society, I think, lies in our tendency to turn the dimensions or qualities of time into synonyms. We use words like age, aging, aged, ageless, and maturity as if they were only slightly different qualities of the same thing. We see them as kinds of set period pieces rather than as reasons for reflection or serious celebration of the purpose and meaning of life. We lose the sense of the spirituality of age, the soulful purpose of life.

But each of these concepts, and all of them, have something different to say about what it means to become whole, about coming to the fullness of the self, about growing in spirit as well as in body.

The fact is that when we collapse these concepts, we eclipse them. Or, truer yet, we obscure and confuse whole phases of our own spiritual development. As in, "I'm 16 and I have the right to have a car." Nothing said, of course, about the character it takes to drive a car. Or, "Well, when you're 50 you deserve respect." No mention of what it requires to really earn respect. Or, "At 65 it's over; there's nothing much a person can do in life now except keep the engine ticking over 'til the battery runs out." No consciousness at all that age itself is one of the great spiritual epochs of life.

That kind of thinking begets a perfunctory and superficial approach to what it means to be alive. It assumes that all of life is merely biological rather than the stuff of the spiritual in its every breath. And yet, any close examination of the language of age itself opens up vast new perspectives about what it means to grow old, to be ageless, to be mature.

"Age" itself, the number of years we bring to the present complex of circumstances, is clearly an indication of little or nothing in the human condition except the inexorable passage of biological time. And even those definitions are loose ones, not to be too strictly defined, not used to guarantee anything. In fact, years tell us very little at all. They do not tell us exactly and surely when people will learn to walk or play, to speak or compute, to love or to lead, to really become mature. Maturity is not simply measured by time or years, grades or civil standards like the legal age for marriage, or drivers licenses, or electability. No, maturity is much more subtle, much more demanding.

Maturity comes from growing through every failure we have ever faced in life and becoming wiser than when we first began. In the mature person we find the determination to become more, ever more, than we now know ourselves to be. In these people we sense an awareness of being called to become everything a fully human individual is meant to be, the best of what each present situation demands.

The process of maturation, then, is a process distilled from failure, from pain, from conviction, from a sense of purpose undeterred, and finally from the ability to persist in the face of futility even when the hoped-for possibility is, at best, more a dream than a reality.

Maturity does not collapse under failure. It does not become hysterical under stress. It does not define success by the accumulation of things or the allure of titles or the trappings of wealth or the garlands of public approval. Maturity is the ripening of emotional stability in the face of emotional loss, in being able to tell the gold from the glitter.

Maturity comes from growing through every failure we have ever faced in life

The mature person brings to life, for all to see, the shining gift of the cultivated soul. There are those who, having lived life through both life's highest heights and its deepest lows, did not seek to escape or deny or wrench these various moments to their own will and at great cost to the lives of everyone around them. Maturity is about being willing to go on growing through every stage of life until the human spiritual compass has been honed to a fine point. These are the people who have something to tell and teach us all.

At that point, at the sight of a person ripened, aged, leavened, and matured, the differences in outlook on age are clear. The pseudo-synonyms of a culture, which have become more defined by time than by human development and wisdom, begin to wither and fail to satisfy.

"Age," we come to realize, as we see more and more of those matured by life rather than merely timed by it, means nothing more than the number of years we've been alive.

"Aging" signifies simply that we all move into different periods of life as we go and are still learning to grapple with each of them. Whether we really will do that well remains to be seen. Whether we accept age as its own spiritual gift and contribution to society makes the difference between aging and becoming aged.

"Aged"—as in "Well, he has certainly ag'ed since the last time

I saw him" — means that, having lived awhile, a person shows the wear and tear of having borne all the twists and turns of life: physical, emotional, and social. We are weathered by the seasons of life and gain the serenity that comes from having survived them all.

"Ag'ed" implies only that a person has lived to be more elderly than most. Whether the number of years lived are themselves enough to make a person the model and gift the rest of humankind seeks depends on the quality of a person's continuing participation in the human enterprise.

Finally, "ageless" suggests that, having lived well for our own time, we have come to transcend the stereotypes of age and become a model now of what it means for a person to live well in all times.

It is to this apex of development that age is meant to bring us. It is the moment in which aging becomes "saging," the moment we

and becoming wiser than
when we first began.

become capable of passing on to generations after us what it means, as Basil of Caesarius taught, to both love God "with your whole heart" and "your neighbor as yourself." But it is also the point of life of which Tennyson speaks when he reminds the older members of society to "strive, to seek, to find, and not to yield" the best of themselves to a sense of futility or uselessness.

On the contrary, it is precisely then, in old age, that we will finally be ready to do what we have been born to do. We will be ready to speak our spiritual truth to those behind us who are still looking for it. And we will be qualified to speak it with courage and conviction. As Louis Kronenberger put it, "Old age is an excellent time for outrage. My goal is to say or do at least one outrageous thing every week."

To be really ripened, to be wholly mature, to make old age worth it, we must make every week of our later lives outrageous ones. •

Growing Down to Earth

Maturity in Meekness

By Joe Grant, MDiv

*Very truly, I tell you, unless a grain of wheat falls into the earth
and dies, it remains just a single grain; but if it dies,
it bears much fruit.* —Jn 12:24

A T THE TENDER AGE of sixteen, my life-call to ministry came
clearly into focus. Already a high-school seminarian, I took
my first paying job assisting the nurses at a geriatric hospital.
Surrounded by aged and dying people, I was brought down to earth
daily by the stark inevitabilities of debilitation, death, and decay.

My first raw encounter with death occurred while I was feed-
ing a patient. Grasping my hand and gazing silently into my eyes,
the elderly man shared his last breath with me. The nurse, who

responded to my frantic calls, comforted me with the prediction that I would never forget this man or this moment of awakening. After decades of theological investigation and spiritual practice, along with several brushes with mortality, loss, and frailty, that first of many awakenings remains powerfully imprinted. That early experience exposed me to the "humus" of our humanity and to the sacredness of shared suffering. It illuminated my life-path as a caregiver and a caretaker. Thereafter, I began in earnest to contemplate the mysteries of growing up and, eventually, growing down toward "earthy" holiness, living into the likeness of "God Most Lowly."

> Everything falls away from us, even memories — even the weariness of self. This is the breaking of the bread, the supreme moment in the prayer of the body, the end of the liturgy of our mortal lives, when we are broken for and in the communion of Christ's love to the whole world.[1]
> — Caryll Houselander

Over the decades, in my attempts at Christian discipleship, certain questions continually surface: *What does a whole life, a "holy" life, look like? What does it mean to be "holy human beings" in a world such as ours? How do "holy people" deal with despair and violence, deprivation and excess?*

In every life there are clear and identifiable stages of development, yet no personal life path is exactly like any other. Some appear to be born aged; "old souls," we call them. Others never quite make it to the so-called "wisdom years." Jesus and other mystical prophets testify that when it comes to wisdom, it is not the years that count, but the mileage — the roads we have traveled. Our unique lives vary widely in their breadth, scope, and depth, and older does not necessarily mean wiser. The latitude of any life is defined in less quantifiable dimensions: the intensity with which we have lived, our deliberate choices, the tragedies we have endured, the failings and disabilities we have integrated. No matter how "seasoned" we are by longevity, there are certain markers for faithful maturity.

> By contrast, the fruit of the Spirit is love, joy, peace, patience, kindness, generosity, faithfulness, gentleness, and self-control. — Gal 5:22–23

Every age, tradition, and culture presents its own variations on a life well-lived. In the Gospels, Jesus invites us to follow his example of holiness, a holiness quite different from the religious and cultural understandings of his (and our) own time. His expansive understanding of a full life goes deeper and wider than having the right ideas, abiding by appropriate religious etiquette, or amassing social (or spiritual) accomplishments. The holiness Jesus embodies is not an invitation to protect ourselves from those places and faces that society deems unclean or unworthy of our attention, nor is he asking us to be piously aloof or fastidious. Instead, the Gospels call out of us a whole, or complete, love.

> One of the scribes came near and heard them disputing with one another, and seeing that [Jesus] answered them well, he asked him, "Which commandment is the first of all?" Jesus answered, "The first is, 'Hear, O Israel: the Lord our God, the Lord is one; you shall love the Lord your God with all your heart, and with all your soul, and with all your mind, and with all your strength.' The second is this, 'You shall love your neighbor as yourself.' There are no other commandments greater than these. —Mk 12:28–31

In Jesus, a completely human life is one in which love for our Maker and care for our neighbor are fused into one inseparable, all-inclusive embrace of life—a full-hearted reconciling, healing, blessed love of enemy, stranger, outcast, sinner, antagonist, and perpetrator (including all of this within ourselves). This is the holiness his followers, the community of disciples, are to embody together. Such holiness is neither easy, nor is it reducible to the individual pursuit of personal perfection. Jesus openly discourages sterile purity and proposes instead an "earthy" humility, lived within a very human caring community. Such holy people have a mission, a clear outlook, a restorative purpose: the healing of our relationships to life.

In his teaching, Jesus discourages us from using our life's breath to theorize our way along a personal trail to glory. We are also warned, in parables and by example, to avoid the traps of self-promoting religious practice: notching up prayer points, seeking personal fulfillment, graduating ourselves through levels of presumed moral ascendency. The holy life is no grand spiritual competition.

When we walk this humbling path together, we are accompanied by a Holy Spirit.

When we engage the Spirit of the Gospels, we are moving in an entirely different direction. We are on a shared journey, an ongoing encounter with "Sacred Mystery," which is both universal hub and cosmic circumference of all relationships. When we walk this humbling path together, we are accompanied by a Holy Spirit. In our coming together we experience the palpable presence of Christ as an intimate connection to suffering-love, love that bonds us together and brings to life the apparent dead spaces between us. When we choose to break open our lives in vulnerability, we can touch and feel the living, breathing, wounded Christ who walks among us.

The learning path we call discipleship is therefore a shared journey in two directions: down and out. Together, we disciples are drawn down into the muck of life, getting our hands dirty with the holy tasks of peacemaking, lifting up what has been put down or cast aside. Together we are sent out to "repair and restore" what has been torn down by engaging injustice with compassion. This is healing work that is worthy of our sacred heritage as God's family, children of the earth.

> For you have looked with favor upon your lowly servant, henceforth all generations will call me blessed. —Lk 1:48

According to Jesus, enlightened or holy living has a definite trajectory toward lowliness or littleness. Paradoxically, he points to children, along with the ones who know they are poor, lost, or forsaken, as the vanguard on our pilgrimage into God's domain. For Jesus and his followers, wisdom is only accessible to those who are small and humble enough to join the meek and the mourning, the poor and the persecuted, in God's "reign of reversals." Blessed humility, the gateway to wisdom, shrinks our self-importance even as it stretches our hearts, so the enlightened Christian (and Christian community) does not try to rise above humanity, but rather aims to embrace it wholeheartedly. According to the upside-down wisdom of the Gospels, muck, meekness, and mercy have more to do with maturity than physical strength, intelligence, age, or social standing.

Many of the stories and parables that appear in the Gospels illustrate this earthiness. Using down-to-earth illustrations from rural life (fig trees, grains, grapes, ravens, sparrows, sheep, and flowers), Jesus depicts our organic connection to creation as expressions of God's goodness. His teachings bring to light a fundamental embrace of our humanness (humus) and creature-hood. Matthew's third beatitude exemplifies his reverence for lowly country folk who, though dispossessed and disdained by the urbane elite, yearn to be at home with the land. Anyone who lives close to the ground knows the tenacity, dedication, and work it demands, as well as the blessings that come from enjoying and sharing the fruits of labor, radiant sunshine, and graceful rain. Such mundane realities are not lost on the majority of people on Planet Earth today. Whether in the campo or shantytown, so many lives still hang in the balance, so many hands turn the soil, so many wait for rain, seek refuge from the storm, and place their hope in providence, and their livelihoods lie in the tenuous turning of the seasons.

...and to walk humbly with your God. —Mi 6:8

The closer we come to the earth, the shorter the distance wisdom has to travel. As we stoop "ground-ward," inclining our hearts to what is small and overlooked, we are graced with wonder in the natural sciences, blessed in contemplating life's awesome mysteries, guided by the ancient learning of indigenous communities. No matter how lofty our buildings or airy our aspirations, when we turn the sod of our spiritual heritage we unearth our authentic identity as holy creatures, part of God's garden. Any attempt to distance ourselves, body and soul, from nature's holy patterns and life-giving interactions only leads to social and spiritual displacement. If we pursue "individual enlightenment," aspire to be above the "dirty," or separate from the "soiled," we risk expelling ourselves from God's good garden. In this earthy Eden, wisdom teaches that things can only grow together, that we can never grow apart.

Have I lived enough?
Have I loved enough?
Have I considered Right Action enough, have I
     come to any conclusion?
Have I experienced happiness with sufficient gratitude?
Have I endured loneliness with grace?

I say this, or perhaps I'm just thinking it.
     Actually, I probably think too much.

Then I step out into the garden,
where the gardener, who is said to be a simple man,
     is tending his children, the roses.[2]

—Mary Oliver

When we alienate ourselves from nature, or live under the influence of a spirit of domination and exploitation, we grow calloused hearts. We mistake the spiritual be-attitude of meekness for weakness. We can grow close to the blessed meekness mandated and lived out by Jesus when we refuse to submit to violence of thought, word, or deed. We can grow down by lowly living, and letting life's seasons, sufferings, and simple joys temper us. Humility opens the door to wisdom, and it is wisdom that mellows the heart.

As I come
to a peaceful awareness
of my limited grasp of truth,
I don't need to defend myself
against people or experiences
which might hold new or challenging information.
I become open to these truths
that reside
half-hidden,
and most often surprising,
in my own

and others' journeys.
And this is a gift
—a rare treasure
freeing me to understand
rather than be understood;
calling me
to fewer words,
to awareness,
to humility,
to patience,
to laughter,
to tenderness,
to listening,
to dancing in the rain,
to waiting on that God
who always
welcomes home
a mellow heart.[3]

—Peter Millar

Reflections on the Spirituality of Aging

By Sally K. Severino, MD

T YPICALLY WE DATE AGING from the moment we are born. The spirituality of aging, therefore, embraces the entire life journey. These are my personal reflections as a woman, mother, and seventy-six-year-old psychiatrist as I ponder our journey through aging.

I once read that all religious traditions say basically the same thing: there is a Divine Reality inherent in the world, our deepest human longing is for this Divine Reality, and our final goal is union with this Divine Reality. That consensus reflects the trajectory of my own spiritual journey of aging, the journey of oneing — of becoming one with God.

In *Sacred Desire* I conceptualized our human longing for Divine

Reality as residing innately within our human personhood, which consists of at least four aspects:[1] biological (including our genetics and biochemistry); psychological and sociocultural (including the actual psychological and sociocultural conditions in which we live plus the personal meanings we make of these conditions); and spiritual (including how we attune to each other and to God). These four aspects of our being are intricately intertwined and influence each other throughout the lifelong process of aging.[2]

Furthermore, each of these aspects may develop more fully—or ripen—at different times of life for different people. For me, the biological and sociocultural aspects ripened rather steadily over the course of my life. The psychological aspect ripened more fully in my twenties, when I began studying psychology, and continued ripening through my retirement from psychiatric practice at age sixty-two. My spiritual aspect ripened more fully from age fifty-eight onward.

I view my remaining life as an opportunity for ever-fuller growth toward union with God, which includes four tasks: honoring endings, making meanings, freeing fear/annulling anger, and giving one's gift.

HONORING ENDINGS

GROWTH TOWARD UNION with God confronts us with many endings. Socioculturally, family and friends die and our circle of relationships narrows with age. Psychologically, we empty as memory diminishes and minds become more fragile. Biologically, we empty as various body parts wear out. Spiritually we empty as our entire being returns to the Source from which we have come, and for which we long with our deepest desire.

It is important to know when something ends and to honor that emptying by letting go. Clinging to the past impedes the spirituality of aging. In the course of my life, endings have presented themselves to me in the following ways:

• Graduation from grade school, middle school, high school, college, and professional training all marked ending points in my formal education. Honoring them, I let them go to enter into lifelong continuing self-education.

- Menopause marked the end of my childbearing capacity. Honoring it, I let it go to live into a body that increasingly became less able to multitask for twenty hours a day.

- The "empty nest" signaled the end of parenting my children. Honoring my children's freedom, I let them go to lead their own lives. I began forming new and different relationships, including relationships with grandchildren.

- I honored retirement by beginning to write books and becoming a Felician Associate, which both broadened my circle of relationships and encouraged my spiritual journey.

Life is a process of emptying and moving into the oneness of life and death. It is living through dying. Honoring endings, with all the sorrow that those "deaths" brings, moves us into joyous freedom. Death is not the final answer.

MAKING MEANINGS

HUMAN BEINGS are meaning-making creatures. Our lives take on new meaning with age. As human longevity has increased, aging no longer means inevitable decline, deterioration, or disability. It is a time to become more authentically ourselves—to be more freely who we really are in the fullness of our ripening.

Spiritually, my childhood entailed baptism and confirmation—a time when I experienced God as parent. During mid-life my relationship with God became an understanding of God as partner. During senior life my relationship with God has taken the form of realizing the oneness of all life, including my journey toward oneness with God. This is consistent with what Swiss psychiatrist Carl Jung described as the seven tasks of aging:

1. accepting death as a part of life
2. reflecting on one's life
3. limiting one's time and energy
4. letting go of ego dominance
5. bringing opposites within us together into wholeness
6. finding meaning in one's life
7. engaging our unused potentials in "dying with life"

In other words, we empty ourselves in imitation of Jesus. When we are totally empty and only God is within us, then we recover our true selves.

When we realize God as our true being, we realize our true selves. All we need to do is open our eyes to the goodness we have possessed all along. In seeing this goodness, we can die to "our" life and live the unique expression of God we were created to be. We can let God act in and through us.

FREEING FEAR/ANNULLING ANGER

W E WILL ALWAYS feel fear and anger because we live in human bodies, but we can live with heroic compassion despite these emotions. Fear and anger change with age. As a child, I feared the dark and became angry if I was told "No." Adulthood carried the fear of not fulfilling responsibilities and brought on anger when I felt thwarted in my strivings. Now in seniorhood, my fears focus on loss—of loved ones, cherished dreams, and physical strength. My anger typically arises in reaction to my sense of impotence.

We can, however, free ourselves from fear and annul our anger by realizing that both emotions occur when we dwell in the past or invent the future. The spirituality of aging invites us to live in the present. It invites us to grieve the past and let go of our perceptions of what the future "should be." By doing so, we don't destroy fear or anger but change our perceptions of them. We welcome their role in alerting us to danger, but free ourselves from their power to determine our actions by putting our bodies into a state of calm, using whatever works for us: prayer, meditation, yoga, exercise, etc. In a body-state of calm, we can allow love to determine our actions. When we can no longer serve the world physically, our prayer can bring compassion into the world.

We are not only the recipients of Divine love; we are also the dispensers of love in the world. When we are one with Christ, our hearts and souls are full of a compassion that then flows out into the world through Christ.

It is important to know when something ends and to honor that emptying by letting go.

GIVING ONE'S GIFT

Each human being is destined to be a unique expression of Christ. I discovered my own unique gift when I was twenty years old and studying in the Philippines. My gift is being a bridge builder whose message is that the kingdom of God is possible when we each take responsibility for using our special gift in the world. In the Philippines I built invisible bridges of international friendships. In midlife, as a mother, I helped my children bridge life's stages into adulthood. As a physician I helped bridge the discipline of psychiatry with the discipline of religion in many different ways, including the establishment of a pastoral care program at the New York-Presbyterian Hospital/Westchester Division. In seniorhood I write books that focus on intersubjectivity: how we are intricately interconnected with one another and all creation.

We are each given the mind of Christ and the ability to give this gift to others. All we need to do is become aware, be grateful, and share our uniqueness with the world around us. Christ encourages us to do as he did—to act freely, expressing our gift in each unrepeatable moment of our lives.

The spirituality of aging is a process of becoming increasingly Christlike–of emptying ourselves until only God lives within us. Just as we are each a unique image of Christ in the world, so too is our ripening process unique. God is always knocking, wanting to enter our lives. All we need to do is open. •

Ripening

By James Finley, PhD

W HEN I WAS a young monk in the monastery of Gethsemani I shared with Thomas Merton that I felt frus-
trated and inept in my efforts to experience God's
presence in my life. In offering an encouraging word, he said, "How
does an apple ripen? It just sits in the sun." He went on to add that
this does not mean that I did not need to continue in my efforts
to seek God. Rather, it means I needed to live in a contemplative
stance of receptive openness to God, achieving in and through my
sincere efforts a spiritual fulfillment that I, by my own efforts alone,
was powerless to achieve. This, it seems, is the intimate and mysterious nature of how we ripen in becoming a mature spiritual person.
We ripen in holiness and spiritual fulfillment as we learn to sit in
the sun of God's mysterious, sustaining presence that energizes and
guides our efforts, bringing us to realms of grace that are beyond,
way beyond, anything we can achieve by our own efforts alone.

The transformative art of ripening occurs in the fundamental
arenas of life. For example, when a young couple gets married, they

look forward to what they hope will be a lifetime of love and happiness together. As the years go by, they ripen as they learn to surrender to a love that guides and fulfills their ongoing efforts to love each other. So, too, with the lifelong process of learning to ripen into a master teacher, or a gifted healer, or a well-seasoned artist or poet, or someone who serves the poor. Those who bless the world in the lifelong process of learning to ripen in such noble endeavors are those who have mastered the art of sustained effort, infused with a surrender to hidden sources of grace that give their efforts a richness or fullness that transcend what their efforts alone could attain.

The lifelong process of ripening brings about a corresponding ripening of our ability to understand the fundamentals in a wiser, peace-giving manner. For example, when people who believe in God go through painful experiences, they are troubled. They say, "If God watches over me, how could God let this happen to me?" This is such an understandable response to suffering in the life of those who trust and believe in God's providential care. However, as a person ripens in unsayable intimacies in God, they ripen in a paradoxical wisdom. They come to understand God as a presence that protects us from nothing, even as God unexplainably sustains us in all things. This is the Mystery of the Cross that reveals whatever it means that God watches over us; it does not mean that God prevents the tragic thing, the cruel thing, the unfair thing, from happening. Rather, it means that God is intimately hidden as a kind of profound, tender sweetness that flows and carries us along in the intimate depths of the tragic thing itself—and will continue to do so in every moment of our lives up to and through death, and beyond.

As fruit ripens, it fulfills itself in reaching its full potential to nurture us and give us pleasure. We might say that, as fruit ripens, it fulfills itself in giving itself to us. In a similar way, we do not undergo the transformative process of ripening for ourselves alone, but rather that our transformed presence might be a source of nurture to others.

Then too, there is the fruit that, in remaining unharvested, falls onto the ground and dies. The lesson here is in Jesus' words, "Unless a grain of wheat falls into the ground and dies, it remains alone, but if it dies, it brings forth fruit a hundred fold, a thousand fold" (John

12:24). And so it is with us. As we grow old we realize that, in all we have been through, Love has been using us for its own purposes. And for this we feel immensely grateful. We know, too, that our inevitable passing away, in which we fall into the ground and die, is not the end of our ripened and transformed life. It is rather our passage into an infinite and deathless fulfillment. Saint John of the Cross talks about a windfall of delight. When fruit becomes very ripe, the slightest wind can cause it to fall to the ground. This is also true of us, and not just in the sense in which we learn to be undone and fulfilled in all the unexpected little blessings that come to us throughout the day. The windfall of delight pertains as well to our last breath, which we know and trust will send us falling forever into the deathless depths of God.

As I end these reflections, what comes to mind is a painting by Paul Cézanne of ripe fruit. Juicy — almost, we might say, voluptuous — with a quiet, nurturing fullness, waiting to be seen, waiting to be eaten and enjoyed. May each of us continue to ripen into this quiet fullness, for God's pleasure, for our own pleasure, and for all whom we might help in any way we can. •

Living in the Light of Death

By Kathleen Dowling Singh, PhD

Aging, illness and death are treasures
for those who understand them.
They're Noble Truths, Noble Treasures.
If they were people,
I'd bow down to their feet every day.
—Ajaan Lee

W E CANNOT SPEAK about aging and awakening without speaking about death and dying. If we hold any intention to awaken, to ripen into the spiritual maturity offered in the unfolding of this precious life, we need to confront our mortality. Opening to our own fleeting impermanence is an act both wise and kind.

This isn't a call to hop on the icebergs, although there probably

Deeply aware of our own impermanence, every fleeting moment is recognized as precious.

occurred deep transformation, deep release into awareness beyond the separate sense of self, for those Inuit elders who, on their tiny islands of ice, floated away from their known world and their loved ones. Perhaps we can think of it as a call to the iceberg experience.

Meditating on death begs us to look at what remains frivolous in our lives, what remains careless and unexamined, where we suffer in our illusions, what beliefs keep us feeling separate from the sacred and from each other. Most of us have lived many decades on the surface of being, whistling around the outskirts of awareness.

Meditating on death is one of the special conditions that facilitates awakening. Wisdom traditions have employed it as skillful means for millennia. It is, at the end of life, one of the most powerful of the special conditions that facilitates the grace in dying. The experience of being changes when the heart takes in the fact of death. Deeply aware of our own impermanence, every fleeting moment is recognized as precious.

Meditating on death instantly calls us to question on the deepest of levels. What am I doing? What do I want? What does this all mean? What is it all about? What is spirit? What is self? Who or what is the "I" that is asking the questions? Our desire to explore, to inquire, to see through the confusion and sense of alienation that have led so much of our lives, amplifies.

Contemplating our own mortality, taking in the fact of our mortality, our precariously impermanent existence, can call us to complete and thorough accountability. It can call us to instant re-ordering of our (mostly unconscious) habits, a rearranging of our priorities and our intentions. It blocks off all of our habitual detours into denial. It forces us to face the way we've lived our lives, the choices we've made, the polestars we've chosen.

Contemplating our own mortality can spur a sense of urgency, an urgency to become more earnest, more sincere, more aligned in the call to awaken. The urgency spurs us to remain mindful of our deepest intention, to no longer allow our experience of being to sink so carelessly into mindlessness.

If we keep the fact of our mortality at the level of conception, in the head, it remains as just another piece of information, like the number of calories in a dish of ice cream or how to plant a tomato seedling. To take in that we will die and that it is uncertain when—that it could be any time, even today—at the level of the heart is an experiential understanding of the whole being that can actually affect and transform us.

When we die, the world the mind experienced will be swept away. It does not endure, just as the passing phenomenon we call "me" does not endure. When we die, all of our thoughts and concerns, all of our prides and attachments, our universe, will cease.

The objects we so loved will be priced for a tag sale, a penny on the dollar. Everything that we are concerned about in this very moment will not matter at all: bills, quarrels, sensed inadequacies, fears, vanities, hopes for the stock market, what to have for dinner. They will not matter at all.

We have spent a long time fretting over, defending, preening, despairing over a sense of self that has always been illusory, a deeply invested concept. Nisargadatta, a profound Indian sage, gives heartfelt advice:

> You have enclosed yourself in time and space,
> squeezed yourself into the span of a lifetime
> and the volume of a body....
> You cannot be rid of problems
> without abandoning illusions.

We *already live* in grace, in the sacred formless. Lost in self, lost in a "form only" paradigm, we miss the sacred formless, always ever present. We have been asleep for so many decades, lost in our deeply-embroidered, dreamlike narratives, paying the price with suffering great and small. We miss the wordless grace, within and around, permeating every moment and every appearance.

Jesus bore witness to awakening from the dream of self. In Gethsemane, he experienced his humanity—aware of his own singularity, aware of self. Even with the depth of his realizations and the magnitude of his love, he experienced the angst of his own impending death.

Jesus prayed, in Gethsemane, the passageway, through the chaotic mind of clinging and reluctance. Surrendering the exclusivity of self-reference—in love, for love, arms wide open on the cross—he emerged into Christ consciousness, transcending the smallness of self, obliterating the separation self imposes.

There is profound beauty in the view, the example, of Jesus' offering, his surrender.

The immensity of his act is worthy of deep reverence and respect, even awe. It doesn't, though, need to cause us to back away from the spiritual journey as if the journey and the arrival are beyond our capacity. His was an encouraging act, not a discouraging one. It would be mistaken to conclude that the journey is something for others who are perhaps more "worthy" or "braver" or "more evolved."

As ordinary beings, it is completely possible, with intention and effort, to free ourselves from the confines of "selfing" in our ordinary lives. It is possible to do this in a completely, beautifully ordinary way. We can do it in our houses, on our streets, within our families. Still voting, still cooking, still waving to the neighbors, shouting "fore" before swinging, and stopping at the stop sign.

As aging beings, we are nearing our expiration date. Future shrinks. Now is the time to awaken, to offer ourselves to ripening, if we have any desire to do so at all.

WE CAN PRACTICE MEDITATING as if we were dying, a profound and skillful way to practice. We can come to intimately know the unfolding stages of chaos, surrender, and transcendence in a frequent contemplation of our own mortality. St. Augustine recognized this when he counseled all who sought his wisdom to "die daily." We ask the meaningful questions. Where am I most deeply attached? Where am I most deeply anxious? What will be lost? What is it that dies?

When we sit to meditate on mortality, we can think that this may be the last time I may ever be able to do this. The power of that thought lies in the fact that the statement holds truth. We can sit to meditate with the intention to imitate death. We can sit to

Where am I most deeply attached?
Where am I most deeply anxious?
What will be lost?
What is it that
dies?

meditate with the intention to let it all go, inspired to explore what lies beyond self.

Although we certainly need a functioning self while in the midst of this lifetime, the belief in a separate, independent sense of self as the shining glory of our potential keeps us small and defended and un-free. We are, in union with the sacred, so much more. The surrender of an illusion buys us entry into grace, immeasurably more than worth the price.

We sit deliberately, with noble posture and noble intention.

We breathe. Progressively, we free our awareness from sensations. We free our awareness from the "I" we imputed upon the sensations and the "mine" with which we tried to claim them. We relieve ourselves of all of our mistaken identifications, loosening our attachments to them, letting them go.

Breathing, we let go of the survival-based need to label all arisings. Dog barking, wind blowing, me meditating. We let go of the labels. Each gives rise to a story and a teller of the story.

Breathing, we let go of the mental images with which we've formed and colored the arisings. We let go of the clinging and aversion to the mental images of our own creation, the mental images which we believe to be external and which we thought would fulfill our neediness or hold our fear at bay, the mental images we hold responsible for our own reactive feeling tones.

Breathing, we free our capacity to believe from our preconceptions and assumptions, self-invested words we've assigned to neural firings.

We completely let go of all that chaos and our attachment to, and identification with, it. We liberate ourselves from illusions and, cleared of all that congested weight, the burden of being a self, we surrender, entering awareness that is spacious and quiet and uncongested.

We just die into silence. Die to the past. Die to the future. Die to the breath. Completely let go. The silence reveals itself as refuge, as awareness that can be trusted, tenderly loving and resounding with the majesty and the mystery of the sacred.

This silence is the practice of absorption, unruffled by even the breath of self, taught in all traditions. To practice it with the recognition that it is similar to the process of dying, to the process of leaving behind attention's entrapment in body and conceptual mind, is to amplify its power.

Such a meditation is about letting go, surrendering—each letting go a death of a mistaken belief. If we want to wake up, we open our eyes. Releasing every illusory prop, we let go into the ripened and hallowed state for which this life was intended.

It is wise and kind to engage in this practice, to enter into the holy sacrament of the defeat of ego's illusions. Living in the light of death, we release our singular attachment to the separate sense of self. With that release, fears of both dying *and* living dissolve.

This skillful means is a method of ripening, of coming to spiritual fruition. Ripened, we can then offer the sweet fruit of the awakened state, every noble quality, to all whom we encounter.

There is no more noble use of this time of our aging. May we all become elders, more than simply old, more than only self. •

Aging From the Contemplative Heart

By *Tilden Edwards, PhD*

S ome of the early Church Fathers well summarized the nature and purpose of our lives when they said that we are born in the image of God and meant to grow into the full likeness of God. I interpret that to mean that our core nature is a unique shaping of divine Spirit energy, a unique shaping of divine love, freedom, and creativity. Given the nature of these three qualities, and our mysterious blindness and willful resistance as well as responsiveness to them, we each live an unpredictable path.

Over time each of us weaves a unique story of responsiveness to the Holy Spirit invitations and divisive spirit temptations of our lives. Each response draws us closer to or further away from consciousness and expression of our true nature in God, the nature of mutually indwelling intimacy shown us in Christ and by great contemplatives over the centuries. Our responses are personal but not private: they are influenced by and influence the larger human story.

Several years ago I developed a simple schema for noticing from where we are listening and responding at a given time. This has increased my and others' awareness of the source of our responses, and offered an opportunity to recognize and give ourselves more fully to the deepest Source.

Let me outline this schema and invite you to see what it's like to discern from where you are listening and responding through the thoughts, feelings, and actions of each day, with the hope that such an awareness will help free you to more often recognize and choose to live from your deep being in God.

I think this schema is consonant with the spiritual anthropology we find in the contemplative heart of Christian scripture and tradition, as well as in the contemplative heart of other deep religious traditions. It is a broad-stroke, abbreviated schema for the sake of practical usefulness; on a theoretical level it could be qualified and expanded a great deal. Although these listening posts inside of us are distinctive (and they could be called by different names than I have chosen), they are not ultimately separate from one another; they are dimensions of one integral personhood.

◆ LISTENING FROM THE LITTLE EGO SELF ◆

This is the conditioned, coping personality dimension of our nature, our "little" self. It is a gift of God that allows us to enjoy and function in the world. However, when we identify with this dimension of self as our ultimate identity, then we can become dominated by its often fearful, over-securing, control-seeking drives and attachments. It can skew our view of the world and limit our

Awareness and cultivation of the contemplative heart as a profound faculty for knowing deep reality has been unrecognized or marginalized.

freedom for Self-in-God centeredness, from which flows our most inclusive, compassionate and direct awareness of reality as it is. When we would rather give ultimate worth to our "little" self-identity, we filter what we hear and how we respond through its narrow self-centeredness.

◆ LISTENING FROM THE THINKING MIND ◆

The mind draws the words we hear and speak through the filter of its learned concepts, categories, images, and values. Our rational and imaginative mind is a great gift of God, including its capacity to recognize and resist our ego's ways of skewing reality. However, if the mind is the ultimate place from which we listen and respond, if we believe its insights bring us fully into the truth, then we have overstepped its capacity. We are in danger of confusing our views with ultimate reality itself. Our concepts then become idols that shrink the great mystery of divine reality to what those concepts can contain, rather than being valuable symbols that point to deep reality beyond the capacity of words and images to fully grasp.

◆ LISTENING FROM THE CONTEMPLATIVE HEART ◆

When we most deeply listen and respond from a third place in us, our spiritual heart, then we more easily avoid the pitfalls of rational idolatry and ego drives, while at the same time respecting the gifted place of rational-imaginative thought and ego functioning in our lives. Our gifted contemplative heart includes our capacity not only to will and intimately feel, but also to "know" deep reality more holistically, intuitively, and directly than our categorizing, thinking minds. In our heart we are immediately present to what is, just as it is, in the receptive space before our thinking mind begins labeling, interpreting, and judging things, and before our ego fears and grasping become operational.

In particularly graced moments we might realize first-hand the mutual belonging of all life together within the dynamic loving wholeness of God. We might realize a spontaneous compassion, free from fear, free to move in any direction called for. We might be given a humble confidence emerging from our awareness of the intrinsic substantiality of this wholeness, a sense of tasting the kin-dom of heaven that is the inmost reality and hope of all that is. We then might find ourselves sharing a little of Jesus' confidence, from which his vision, words, and acts flowed.

My interpretation of the early Christian desert elders' over-encouragement of allowing the mind to sink to the heart is that the mind needs to bathe in the contemplative heart's more naked availability to the gracious Presence, from whence the mind's fun-damental spiritual insights emerge.

As our spiritual journey proceeds in grace, yearning, and will-ingness, we find our egos and our thinking, imaging, and subcon-scious minds, along with our bodily senses, more and more free to be vessels of the communing, loving Light shown us in our contempla-tive hearts, albeit never completely in this life.

The flow of this liberating, living Light slowly melts away many of the attachments in us that divide us from our true being in God. In our awareness of forgetful, agitated, and willful/sinful times, we become more accepting of the forgiving and encouraging love and image-of-God dignity that is ours as we turn to the gracious Presence. That dignity still lives in our core being right through every physical and mental disability that we might endure in life.

Let me give you a concrete example of one expression of such spiritual maturity, showing itself in this case at the end of life. Thomas Hand, a Jesuit friend, spent 29 years in Japan as a mission-ary, where he discovered the value of Zen practice for the deepening of contemplative awareness. He became a Christian Zen teacher and retreat leader in this country after his retirement. In my times with him on retreat and in personal conversation over the years, I found him full of those three divine attributes I mentioned at the beginning which define the image of God in us: communing love, freedom, and creativity. Here is a selection from a letter he sent to his friends after he discovered his terminal cancer:

hidden divine radiance shining in us and all creation.

I seem to grow a bit weaker each day. But I am peaceful and happy…. I've been saying to people that God has manifested in me in my good health for over 80 years. It has been great. Now God wants to manifest in even my terminal illness and that is great, too.

Please do pray for me as you feel moved. I will continue to pray for you all. What I really want is to become the Flow of the Spirit. My desire is to fully enter into the movement of Reality. No scenarios about what's to come. Just live the Now…. To be very honest, it's all quite exciting (can't think of a better word). All I want is that it be a time of transformation.

Tom's spiritual maturity was fed above all by his enduring desire for it. It was also fed by his contemplative practices that by grace brought him to his little-self-emptied spiritual heart and helped him remember and embrace his deepest identity and freedom in the gracious One Who Is. His maturity was aided also by a responsive spiritual community of heart-centered believers and seekers, and by a reading of scripture and the saints with the eye of his heart.

The widespread contemplative re-awakening in recent decades in which Tom was a participant is, I believe, a Spirit-inspired response to the wide scale shrinkage of our identity and capacity to ego, mind, and feelings alone in what has been taught about our human nature in both Western religious bodies and secular culture over the past 500 years. Awareness and cultivation of the contemplative heart as a profound faculty for knowing deep reality has been unrecognized or marginalized. Many clergy and laity alike, as well as those unconnected with any organized religion, yearn for something more than they've normally been given in terms of understanding the mutually indwelling intimacy of human and divine nature and the path to its incarnate fullness. It's an intrinsic God-given longing to realize the hidden divine radiance shining in us and all creation.

The rise of contemplative practices today stems from this haunted place in us all—from the desire to grow more fully into who we really are. We need to cultivate spiritual communities of people and wise leaders who share this preeminent desire: communities where there is mutual support, challenge, and practices to foster the lifetime journey from the image to the likeness of God. What emerges from such communities will spill over into the world's life, as they become aware of the shared transcendent ground that contemplative awareness can bring to all dimensions of societal life. Listening and responding together from the contemplative heart in all societal settings can further the maturing of human relationships, purpose, and inclusive societal well-being: the ripening of the communal kin-dom of heaven. •

Tilden Edwards says more about the spiritual heart in his book, *Embracing the Call to Spiritual Depth: Gifts for Contemplative Living* (Paulist Press, 2010.).

The Stone Rejected

By Mark McGonigle, MAS, LCSW

M Y BODY CLENCHED up as I sat before a messy desk, shoulders hunched, fear creeping up my neck and pulsing through my jaw — why was the simple task of documenting psychotherapy notes so hard? Midlife found me in this state in 2005 — a well-respected psychotherapist, known for being soothing, yet I still gnawed my fingernails. I was unable to reach a part of myself that was very much stuck in fear, anxiety, and dread. More than I knew at the time, I was living a half-life, avoiding my own vitality, not authoring my own life.

I was sent to receive training in EMDR (Eye Movement Desensitization and Reprocessing), purported to be a rapid process of healing trauma. Francine Shapiro discovered in 1988 that side-to-side eye movement facilitated reprocessing of memory, removing the emotional and cognitive sting of trauma.

In my training I was invited to identify an issue, person, or event in my current life that was moderately stress-inducing. I chose my messy desk and my documentation tardiness. I was asked to visualize the stressor, and then tune in to my feelings, especially as they resonated in my body. I was gently led to breathe and observe my body and its response. I felt the stress intensely in my shoulders, like the talons of a bird of prey grabbing me. Then, while attending to my body, I was invited to allow another part of my mind drift into the past.

Suddenly I was standing in my fourth-grade classroom. Sister Cecilia, a tall and skinny Irish nun, was standing over me. She had caught sight of my desk. The cubby underneath my seat was burgeoning with trash—old lunches, notebooks with bent spirals, chewed pencils, and an avalanche of random papers. She stopped, grabbed me by the shoulder, and forced me out of my seat. Picking up the desk over her head, and dumping its contents, she screamed, red-faced, "The city dump!!" Immediately my observing mind felt the connection in my adult body. I was still that little, skinny, confused, and disorganized nine-year-old boy struck with terror.

I was in the perfect spot to begin reprocessing. My eyes followed the provider's finger, moving left and right in slow rhythm. I was plunged into a vivid recall of the emotions of my school days. I felt the deep loneliness of the "out of step" student, the eighth of nine children, with nobody to talk to about my struggle to be good enough. I overflowed with convulsing sobs and tears, and at the same time there was a deep vibration or pulsing in my being, as waves of energy flowed through and around me. I was staying close to myself, in a way that I never could have done when Sister

I discovered
a divine inner self,
pushing at the walls of my ego,
like a chick longing
to hatch...

Cecilia was screaming. I felt a deep satisfaction that I was returning to something lost and rejected, but essential. I was entering a journey into my own being that had eluded me well into midlife. At the end of this emotional storm there was a profound calm, an absence of inner noise, and a sense of wholeness. I was convinced of the method's efficacy and my need. After my training, I sought out a therapist to continue the process.

What I have gained since is a new way to see myself. Everything I am today is a memory—for good and for ill. Every skill I possess, every bit of self I claim as solid, reliable, and full of integrity, was built through memory. So when I wake each morning, moving out of dream states into conscious living, my brain accesses the consolidated memory of who I am, where I am, what I do, and what it all means.

But I also awake every morning with my body full of exiled versions of myself, outside the usual narrative of my life. I am carrying various stories, and traumatic memories are at the core of my inner pariahs. My emotions and bodily stress are the places where I can meet and greet these orphans, created at painful moments in time when my caregivers could not meet my needs for emotional support. I subsequently had weak skills for attuning to my inner world. I even discovered that some memories had a built-in automatic response of disconnection, my body numbing and my mind dimming. I learned to journey through that fog into intimate encounters with myself.

I learned that trauma had set in due to a shutdown of reprocessing in the wake of emotional pain and threat. I lacked the internal and external resources for mindful presence to myself. The initial stored experience lived on in its original state, with all of the sensory data, sense of embodiment, and distorted reactive thoughts. These memories live on in an inner state of exile, vulnerably associating themselves with the present circumstances and flooding the body with old stuck feelings.

I am always telling myself a story about me. But many memories were frozen in their original states, lurking in my body, easily triggered, and I had been avoiding them for decades.

I discovered that the storytelling process has a few simple rules encoded into my brain.

- I am not allowed to leave any version of myself out of my story.

- My most difficult moments are the most important and valuable.

- These events, given the right attention, can and will change their shapes and meanings over time.

- My story and its elements want to take a shape that is heroic, triumphant, meaningful, and transcendent.

- My story takes place in the cosmos as it is, lovingly observed by my Creator. I am never alone.

And herein lay the problem—my traumatic memories were breaking all of the rules. They seemed useless and as if they had no place in the story. The memories were stuck and never changed their shapes or meanings. I wanted to get rid of them, but they intruded at the worst moments with a sense of doom, defeat, and slavery. They were the "stone rejected by the builders" (Acts 4:11–12), those useless pathetic moments of my life. Couldn't I just pretend they did not happen, discard them as useless, insist to myself that I didn't feel them? Couldn't I just figure it out, muscle through, and rise above?

That rejected stone became the cornerstone of a new self, weaving in more of the lost parts with a renewed sense of wonder, openness, and discovery. I discovered that my traumas were actually entire worlds of learning that I had unwittingly deferred. I had become stuck in a state of non-learning and my story was taking a dark turn—darker and more dangerous than I'd realized. I found out how hard I had been working on the inside to keep those events and memories out of my story. I was a defensive person, guarding my ego from the insults of the past. My body was bearing the burden.

Throughout the work, my brain began healing itself. There was a pattern imposed by neither my therapist nor me which was led from within. I learned to ride waves of emotions, to stay close to my body, to reconnect to old lost versions of myself. I was seeing into the corners of my memory. For three years, I regularly sat with my therapist and rewrote whole chapters of my life. I reprocessed cruelty and scarcity of attachment in my family, fears absorbed in my religious upbringing, deep shame, fear, and suspicion of my own body, failed attempts at love, and repetitive self-induced misery. Somewhere along the way I lost my compulsion to bite my nails.

Through all of this I became aware of the confines of my own ego. It was a shell largely constructed to protect me from threats to my wounded self. I discovered a divine inner self, pushing at the walls of my ego, like a chick longing to hatch, hoping to dance on the broken shell and stretch out its wings.

I now have a new view of the last half of my life. I want to be a masterful storyteller. I will continue to tell myself about my life and find beauty, compassion, triumph, and transcendence in the tragedies of the past. I will learn right up to the end. I feel the resilience in my body. Anything that happens, past, present, or future, is an opportunity for learning. I will help others do the same, in any way I can. I will listen to their stories and trust in their innate ability to learn from the discarded lessons of the past. Love will be real.

Can the human family depart from our traumatized state of non-learning? I am hopeful. If we look with compassion and curiosity into the pain of our bodies, we can include everything in our stories. Our own bodies will lead us if we follow. We can find the rejected stones, and start building right in the middle of our lives — maybe just in time. •

Old Age:
Journey into Simplicity
by Helen Luke

Reviewed by Joelle Chase

We shall not cease from exploration
And the end of all our exploring
Will be to arrive where we started
And know the place for the first time.
— T.S. Eliot

W E ARE A STORIED species, humans. From the rich aural tradition prior to written language, to pictographs on rock walls, to literature ancient and modern, stories have given us meaning and purpose. Jungian analyst Helen Luke knew this well — that beyond their power to teach and entertain, stories carry deep wisdom of universal archetypes that could otherwise go forgotten, hidden in the individual subconscious.

Stories open the doors to possibility, helping us find new — yet familiar — ways of being that are in harmony with our authentic selves and the natural evolution of a life.

In the tradition of a *cantadora*, Luke is guide and way-finder through four stories particularly relevant to the theme of ripening. Her book, *Old Age: Journey into Simplicity*, reflects on the final journeys within four texts: Homer's *Odyssey*, Shakespeare's *King Lear* and *The Tempest*, and T.S. Eliot's *Little Gidding*. It is a small book, not a tome, for Luke writes of a time in life when words eventually become superfluous, and those who are going gently will already know, having been led and transformed by living and by Life itself, of what she writes so simply. But for many these reflections may be just the wedge in the door needed to open themselves to the gifts of aging or, at the least, may give context and comfort for what can be a disconcerting, lonely time of letting go.

Luke follows the footsteps of maturing ego and soul in each story, interpreting them as a wildlife tracker might tell the tales of paw prints:

- Here, where Odysseus sat looking at the ocean, dreaming of further adventure and conquest; where he remembered the blind seer's prophecy and regretted his own violence disguised as valor; this is where his choice was made — to obey the call of the further journey, inland, carrying a tool useless for this kind of voyage, an oar, to be planted, and blossom, and bear fruit forever.

- There, in the sing-song tone of King Lear's voice, calling to his daughter Cordelia to come away with him to prison, welcoming weakness, dimmed sight, faded hearing, loss of purpose; this is where he became God's spy, "one who sees at the heart of every manifestation of life…the *mysterium tremendum* that is God."

- This place, on the island where Prospero's enemies are at the mercy of his spells, the wizard learns humility, releasing the powers he's created, letting reality be what it is, and finds the courage to forgive others and self — "in this moment of forgiveness all one's sins and weaknesses are included, being at the same time both remembered and known as the essential darkness which has revealed to us the light."

Like a poet, Luke uses words sparingly to create a framework, leaving space for her reader's imagination and intuition to fill in the details. Perhaps there is even more wisdom in what she leaves unsaid. Indeed, one of the gifts of moving toward death is emptiness. Luke writes of the paradox of Christ on the cross, completely empty, yet simultaneously filled with the wholeness of God. It is an "emptiness that is the Mercy, the Compassion, which contains all opposites." Prospero's Ariel—"that gift which we recognize as inborn and not learned"—has been freed and is "happily superfluous" now, and yet also a unique and essential part of the great web of exchange that is the universe of "cosmogonic love." After a lifetime of separating—self from other, good from bad—the oneing commences in earnest, reuniting the split and scattered pieces within Love, which is infinitely spacious.

Though I am likely far from this stage in my own story (I cannot yet release my Ariel from his duties to inspire my ego "to bring to fruition in this world his image-making power"), I read Luke's reflections with great anticipation. I'm willing to let the ripening take its sweet time, but hopeful that when my final journey begins, I, like Odysseus, Lear, and Prospero can accept what Eliot calls "A condition of complete simplicity/(Costing not less than everything)" and surrender into this mystery:

And all shall be well and
All manner of thing shall be well
When the tongues of flame are in-folded
Into the crowned knot of fire
And the fire and the rose are one.
                              —T.S. Eliot

Dreams and the Stages of the Soul

By Harry R. Moody, PhD

T HE SPIRITUAL JOURNEY unfolds over time, as mystics down through the ages have told us. Too often, we identify our journey with waking consciousness. Yet the great wisdom traditions of the world remind us that our dreams, too, are stations along the journey of the soul, as I have tried to show in *The Five Stages of the Soul.*

THE CALL

M edard Boss tells of the case of a woman who had been "spiritually and emotionally blind" all her life. Her interests were strictly limited to what was pragmatic or material. Then one night she received "the call." It came to her in a dream about a Franciscan monk, who had travelled around the world as a wandering preacher, finally returning to a monastery as his time on earth drew to an end:

I was in this monastery nursing him. He lay in his bed and he had a very spiritual face. The room was friendly. It was lit by the golden glow of the evening sun and I asked the monk to tell me the true relationship between man, truth, and God. I told him that I knew of his omniscience, and that I felt he could tell me. He answered that what we men saw and imagined as reality and truth was a mere fabrication of our own desires and instincts. It was a stage prop, hiding, distorting and diminishing the divine truth within us. After he said this, he died.[1]

This classic dream came "out of the blue," but it conveyed a powerful message to the dreamer. The Franciscan friar in this dream evidently represents the unfulfilled spiritual aspiration of the dreamer herself, an aspiration that she is "nursing" or caring for, even at a time in her life when she is consumed in materialism. In the dream she asks the friar all her deepest questions. The message that she receives is not any particular doctrine but rather a "wake up call," namely, a message that everything we see around us is "a mere fabrication of our own desires."

THE SEARCH

T HE SEARCH often requires that we come to a new understanding of the religion in which we have come of age. Viktor Frankl, creator of logotherapy, cites the dream of a patient who, on her way to the psychiatrist's office, passed by a particular church. She would often think to herself that she was on her way to God, not through the church directly but instead through psychotherapy. Going to therapy was, in a sense, a "detour" to the church. Then in a dream she found herself entering the very same church she often used to pass in waking life:

The church seems deserted. The church is entirely bombed out; the roof has fallen in, and only the altar remains intact. The blue heavens shine through here; the air is free. But above me is still the remainder of the roof, beams that threaten to fall down, and I am afraid of that. And I flee into the open, somewhat disappointed.[2]

"...the more conscious we become as individuals, the more hope there is for our tiny portion of the universe."

Frankl notes that the seeming desertion of the church in this dream really suggests that it is the dreamer who has deserted the church. The imagery of the dream begins to tell us why. Her familiar religious faith is portrayed in the dream as merely a shell, a structure that is "bombed out," with its "roof fallen in." "Only the altar remains intact." The altar, of course, is the center of spiritual life, where the divine mystery unfolds. Above this mysterious center is the path to what is transcendent: the "blue heavens" and the free air. Frankl suggests that the remaining beams of the structure threaten to fall down on this dreamer because she is afraid of, once again, being trapped in the debris of a religion that is only a wrecked shell of what it is supposed to be.

Interestingly, the dreamer of "the deserted church" had actually experienced ecstatic mystical states.

THE STRUGGLE

THE STAGE of the soul called "the struggle" demands that we face up to something in ourselves that is our enemy, yet also part of us. This psychological truth was conveyed in Robert Louis Stevenson's *Dr. Jekyll and Mr. Hyde*. Like Jekyll and Hyde, these two opposing parts of the self are actually one and the same person, while to our waking minds they seem to be separate; the struggle is to see them as one.

We see the struggle in the following dream from Carl Jung's patient, Anna Marjula, as cited by Barbara Hannah. The dream appears in Marjula's own account of her very long therapeutic process aimed at dealing with deep neurotic issues in her life. After many years of struggle, she had the following powerful dream, rich with religious imagery:

The patient approaches a big building. A nun comes out of it, welcomes her and gives her a rosary which consists of only a few beads. Every bead is a prayer. The nun tells her to thread more beads onto that rosary, black beads, which will become brilliant and radiant as soon as she has threaded them.[3]

In her association with the beads (prayers) in this dream, Marjula said that they were called "humility, poverty, and fasting with the heart"—that is, classical Christian virtues. She specifically associated poverty with evocative words from Rilke's meditative *Book of Hours*. In this dream, the figure of the nun represents a kind of ego ideal or spiritual self toward which Marjula aspired, hoping for this to be her own fate. Barbara Hannah suggests that the black beads of the rosary constituted elements of the patient's shadow, or unacknowledged parts of herself, parts which could eventually become "brilliant and radiant" as soon as she had "threaded them" (i.e., brought them fully into consciousness).

The wounds of childhood were still all too evident in Marjula's life. It would be years before she could "hear" the deep truth of this dream: namely, that it would be necessary for her, in Marion Woodman's phrase, to "descend into the basement," to go down into the "foul rag and bone shop of the heart." In the opening image of the dream, Marjula has indeed approached "a very big building," namely, a huge structure or life task, nothing less than the immensity of her own unconscious, out of which the nun has emerged. The nun gives her a rosary consisting of only a few beads: namely, those very few tasks that are necessary, and unavoidable, as part of the dreamer's fate. There is no way of rising to a "higher" spiritual plane—or becoming, in Woodman's dream, a "priestess of the temple"—without going down into the lower level of the basement. This was the struggle in which this dreamer was engaged.

BREAKTHROUGH

THE STAGE of the soul called "the struggle" may be followed by a glimpse of what gives us hope and meaning. The following dream is from a middle-aged man who had sought meaning in his life through psychotherapy. He worked through psychological issues but remained perplexed by what traditionally has been understood to be the problem of evil. This dreamer, like Job, asked the question, "Why me? Why have I been tested?" Then came a glimpse of transcendence:

> It was night and I was alone. I noticed some light and as I looked up at the sky I saw many circles of light moving and whirling through the sky. As they moved they gave off rays of light. I stood and watched them for some time; there were many of them and they were very beautiful.[4]

In the dream, the dreamer is alone and it is nighttime: the darkness around him is a symbol of his profound isolation and darkness of spirit. This is the aspect of the struggle which St. John of the Cross called "The Dark Night of the Soul." But a sign of grace is present. The dreamer notices circles of light in the sky, an image reminiscent of Van Gogh's painting "Starry Night," which represents an aspiration toward transcendence felt by the Dutch painter, another tortured soul. The dreamer recognizes the tremendous beauty in these circles of light in the sky, which are like the angelic figures, or luminous souls, in "Paradiso," the third and final part of Dante's Divine Comedy.

THE RETURN

A "BREAKTHROUGH" DREAM is a "big dream," but it is not a gift for the dreamer alone. As Joseph Campbell says, "A myth is a public dream; a dream is a private myth." The stage of "The Return" demands that we bring together the public and private worlds.

Dag Hammarskjöld was one of the most admired figures of the 20th century. Known to the wider world as Secretary General of the United Nations, he acted on the world stage as a diplomat and peacemaker. In 1965 his diary, Markings, was published; the book chronicled his deep introspection and mystical devotion. Hammarskjöld had evidently gone through the stages of the soul, including the stage of "the return." Here is one of his dreams as recorded in Markings:

> In a dream I walked with God through the deep places of creation; past walls that receded and gates that opened

through hall after hall of silence, darkness and refreshment—the dwelling place of souls acquainted with light and warmth—until, around me, was an infinity into which we all flowed together and lived anew, like the rings made by raindrops falling upon wide expanses of calm dark waters.[5]

Over and over again in *Markings*, we find clear expressions of the stages of the soul, from call, search and struggle into breakthrough, as for example in this passage:

In the point of rest at the center of our being, we encounter a world where all things are at rest in the same way. Then a tree becomes a mystery, a cloud a revelation, each man a cosmos of whose riches we can only catch glimpses. The life of simplicity is simple, but it opens to us a book in which we never get beyond the first syllable.[6]

How do we reconcile this intense inwardness, this profound spiritual orientation, with the fact that Hammarskjöld spent his days in a whirlwind of meetings with personalities like Eisenhower and Khrushchev, among many others? Hammarskjöld had clearly reached the stage of breakthrough but this was for him the basis for action in the world: "...our work for peace must begin within the private world of each one of us. To build for man a world without fear, we must be without fear... How can we ask others to sacrifice if we are not ready to do so?"[7] In his dream, we see the link between "the dwelling place of souls acquainted with light and warmth" and what Hammarskjöld accomplished on the worldly stage.

Consideration of dreams and "the return" leads us to appreciation of the importance of dreaming, not only for individual psychology or self-realization, but for the wider society, as Anthony Stevens has noted: "To work on dreams, therefore, is not a petty form of self-indulgence, but a spiritual ritual of cultural and ecological significance: the more conscious we become as individuals, the more hope there is for our tiny portion of the universe."[8] •

Aging and Spirituality

By W. Andrew Achenbaum, PhD

BETTE DAVIS WAS RIGHT: aging is not for sissies. Late life can be difficult and trying. Bodies wear out. Minds decay. Drinking and drugs do not relieve all suffering. Expectations go unfulfilled; friends and family let us down. Losses mount. Elders generally prefer not to rely too much on the kindness of strangers or to suffer fools for too long. Loneliness, self-imposed or otherwise, heightens our vulnerability and insecurity. Older persons usually are resigned to accept that dying is part of living but, as the hour of death approaches, most of us wonder (often fearfully) about what's next.

No wonder growing older provokes discomfiting questions. What meaning do our lives (still) hold? What remains worthwhile? How much difference have we made in others' lives? Have we been faithful stewards and loving neighbors?

Peace, sissies; aging well can be rewarding in richly unexpected ways. Advancing years provide chances for rekindling relationships with intimates, including God. Our last acts may sustain hopes for a fruitful, peaceful finale.

Aspects of my spiritual journey might parallel yours, but our stories probably diverge greatly. At 66, I can at last take off my mask—there is little to hide. Regrets over having spent too little time listening to soul-mates or talking about what matters do not preclude opportunities for trying again and again. I believe that a loving, transcendent, immanent God gives everyone the grace and courage to ripen. Elders have time to celebrate the beauty of creation and, if they choose, to join Saint Francis in kissing the leper that dwells within us and others.

CR ℘

I N MY MIND'S EYE I still see the sunlight streaming through the sacristy window. I am twelve, newly confirmed, a recently-trained acolyte. An aura illuminates the priest as he leads servers in reciting excerpts from Psalms 42 and 43 prior to services. "As a deer longs for flowing streams, so my soul longs for you, O God (42:1)." I have no difficulty identifying with the psalmist insofar as adolescence makes me feel like a buck. Postwar American material-ism quenches my thirst. Cold-war fears cannot shake my conviction that God is a Marine, *semper fidelis*.

I did not pine then for a deeper relationship with God. Good fortune extended through early years of marriage, the birth of two children, and academic success. Forgetting Dante, at age 40 I entered into the dark woods unaware of imminent danger. That I somehow coped with the unexpected deaths of four loved ones did not prepare me to wrestle with demons of my own making.

Tragedy cut me down to size. Psychiatrists consigned me, thus far privileged, among "them." I suddenly had become someone to be treated at a distance from stags. My response to suffering paled beside Job: I neither emulated his faith nor shared that protago-nist's desire to meet God face to face. Much remained the same, but things were different. I wanted something more. As the Yiddish proverb put it, "If you have nothing to lose, you can try everything." I decided to start anew.

I purposively set out on a spiritual journey to satiate my inner longings. I read psalms. I encountered spiritual beacons—Francis and Catherine of Assisi, Hildegard of Bingen and Julian of Norwich, George Herbert, and William Blake. Thomas Merton's writings directed me to Eastern mystics. Deliberately emulating Dorothy Day's ministry, I volunteered at homeless shelters.

All of this, I recall, proved edifying, heady, and hope-filled. Looking back, these spiritual activities embodied where I had been and pointed to where I intended to head. None of these spiritual endeavors pierced my heart, however. Relying on self-generated "enthusiasm" no longer worked. Planting feet on a spiritual path did not empower me to engage a friend in soul-talk.

How serendipitous, then, to receive a copy of Rumi's poetry as I stumbled into the second half of life. Initially I wondered how the dreams and shadows of a 13th century Muslim related to me. I quickly found in Rumi a soul mate who knew how to romance God. Rumi embodied how lovers extolled the Extraordinary in essentially earthy ways:

> Not Christian or Jew or Muslim, not Hindu,
> Buddhist, sufi, or zen. Not any religion....
>
> I belong to the beloved, have seen the two
> worlds as one and that one call to and know,
>
> first, last, outer, inner, only that
> breath breathing human being.
>
> —Rumi, "Only Breath"[1]

Rumi taught me to conjoin religious commitments with spiritual peregrinations. Living his verses animated my attempts to integrate thoughts, feelings, and deeds. For the first time in my life I ached to become whole. I longed to draw nearer to a Presence that I only dimly perceived was all around me.

For the past quarter-century—after surviving cancer and coming to terms with divorce and other losses—I have tried to reconcile work and play, professional and personal spheres. To retrofit my past, I spent three years with a postdoc writing an essay, "On

...God
gives everyone
the grace and courage
to ripen.

Becoming Job." I adopted Rumi for a "spirituality and aging" course I teach to social workers. I assisted several local organizations that promote interfaith dialog and outreach. I savored heartfelt times with kindred spirits. With gratitude I have learned to treasure silence as I contemplated the Ineffable.

Psalm 42 remains a favorite psalm; I finally appreciate how deep waters refresh life. Over time Psalm 139 has become another cherished anchor. Despite the inevitable lapses and dry spells, I give thanks for exchanges with One who can always "discern my thoughts from far away." Old habits die hard: I continue vainly to struggle to perfect myself. And yet, I can let go and surrender to a God who knows me, warts and all. "Such knowledge is too wonderful for me.... I praise you, for I am fearfully and wonderfully made" (Ps 139:6, 14). Love, I discovered late, (but not too late) animates all creation; it trumps childish ambitions and mid-life entitlements. Love empowers me to love, share, and forgive. Confronting demons and shadows remains painful business; I sulk and founder before I pray in hard times. Yet proceeding on a spiritual path, albeit provisionally, assures me that I am never utterly alone, estranged or rejected.

CB 80

ND SO A PARADOX permeates spiritual aging: While every individual's story is unique, "there is nothing singular" in how the vicissitudes of age summon life's bedrock truths.[2] Although contingencies and misfortune etch particularities in everybody's journey, we all must die. How we measure our days hinges on how each self faces cumulative sufferings.

Aging in the shadows of finitude entails renewal, not rejuvenation. Growing older nurtures and sustains human growth—if we are present to life's possibilities and God's mysteries. Ideally, spiritual aging interconnects minds, hearts, and movements in authentic ways. Conscious aging engenders spiritual ripening and vice versa, ripening into an integrity that surpasses our former selves.

The process of spiritual aging is never complete. Wisdom quests remain works in progress. Three truths, nonetheless, sustain this pilgrim longing for an omniscient, omnipresent God.

1. Life, by turns chaotic and enlightening, gets more precious in maturity.

2. Spiritual gifts are bestowed, not earned. Some arrive in dark nights. Some serendipitously resemble epiphanies.

3. Those vulnerable enough to discern the abundance of creation see Love everywhere.

Aging is not for sissies. Spiritual aging offers grounds for hope, yet it is no shield from wounds. Spirituality promises a way to strip away impediments (including transitory assets) that keep us from celebrating connections with an Ultimate Reality who loves us and wants us to love others. Some sojourners grasped this fundamental truth as children. Others (including me) denied or ignored the insight in adulthood. Fortunately, spiritual aging is not a competition with staging platforms and digital timers.

Perhaps this is why elders so often become pacesetters in spiritual aging. Distinguishing kairos from chromos, older seekers find time—and make time—to surrender to God with thanks and confidence. Whereas hard knocks invariably beset the living, untold blessings teach us that life is more than a veil of tears. To be fully human is to embrace the serendipitous, unexpected twists of mature faith and fate.

Spiritual elders who thirst for living waters often discover that reservoirs overflow, spilling into other fountains and cisterns. God's life-giving abundance exceeds material riches. The well-spring of spiritual aging, miraculously, always remains just within our reach. ◆

NOTES

Introduction

1 Richard Rohr, *Falling Upward: A Spirituality for the Two Halves of Life* (San Francisco: Jossey-Bass, a Wiley Imprint, 2013), xvi–xxix.

2 Richard Rohr, *The Naked Now: Learning to See as the Mystics See* (New York: The Crossroad Publishing Company, 2009), 108–115.

Learning to Live Well for the Sake of Those Who Have Yet Lived Little

1 Alfred, Lord Tennyson, *Poems*, 2 vols. (Boston: W. D. Ticknor, 1842). PR 5550 E42a Victoria College Library (Toronto).

Growing Down to Earth: Maturity in Meekness

1 Maisie Ward, *Caryll Houselander: That Divine Eccentric* (London: Sheed and Ward, 1962), 319.

2 Mary Oliver, *A Thousand Mornings: Poems* (New York: The Penguin Press, 2012), 7.

3 Peter Millar, *The Surprise of the Sacred: Finding God in Unexpected Places* (Norwich: Canterbury Press, 2004), 141–142.

Reflections on the Spirituality of Aging

1 Nancy K. Morrison, MD and Sally K. Severino, MD, *Sacred Desire: Growing in Compassionate Living* (West Conshohocken, PA: Templeton Foundation Press, 2009), 21–22.

2 Ibid., 104–107.

Old Age: Journey into Simplicity

1 Helen M. Luke, *Old Age: Journey into Simplicity* (Barrington, MA: Lindisfarne Books, 2010), 30.

2 Ibid., 46.

3 Ibid., 89.

4 Ibid., 49.

5 Ibid., 87.

6 Ibid., 43.

7 T.S. Eliot, *Four Quartets* (New York: Mariner Books, 1968).

Dreams and the Stages of the Soul

1 Boss, Medard, *The Analysis of Dreams* (New York: Philosophical Library, 1958), 134–135.
2 Frankl, Viktor E., *Man's Search for Ultimate Meaning* (New York: Barnes and Noble Books, 2000), 50–52.
3 Hannah, Barbara, *Encounters with the Soul: Active Imagination as Developed by C.G. Jung* (Wilmette, IL: Chiron, 1981), 152.
4 McDonald, Phoebe, *Dreams: Night Language of the Soul* (New York: Continuum, 1985), 218, 100.
5 Hammarskjold, Dag, *Markings* Leif Sjoberg and W.H. Auden (trans.) (London: Faber and Faber London, 1964), 100.
6 Ibid., 148.
7 United Nations, *UN Press Release SG/360*, December 22, 1953.
8 Stevens, Anthony, *Private Myths: Dreams and Dreaming* (Cambridge, MA: Harvard University Press, 1995), 353.

Aging and Spirituality

1 Coleman Barks, trans. *The Essential Rumi, New Expanded Edition* (New York: HarperOne, 2004), 40.
2 Jeanne Murray Walker, "A Conversation with Christian Wiman," *Image*, Issue 76 (Winter 2013), 52.

Center for
Action and
Contemplation

Home of THE ROHR INSTITUTE

A collision of opposites forms the cross of Christ.
One leads downward preferring the truth of the humble.
The other moves leftward against the grain.
But all are wrapped safely inside a hidden harmony:
One world, God's cosmos, a benevolent universe.